T0303686

DOLLHOUSE

DOLLHOUSE

poems by Elaine Terranova

Off the Grid Press

Somerville, Massachusetts

Off the Grid Press
24 Quincy Street
Somerville, MA 02143
http://offthegridpress.net

See the acknowledgments page at the end of this book for publication citations and notes on the poems.

Cover photograph: "Kitchen of tenant purchase client. Hidalgo County, Texas," by Russell Lee (1903–1986). Library of Congress, Prints & Photographs Division, FSA/OWI Collection, LC-USF34- 032145-D

Printed by Cushing-Malloy, Inc., Ann Arbor, Michigan. Author photograph by Dennis Gingell. Book design by Michael Alpert.

To JoAnn and Nelson

and to Lee

*I wonder about the world in which this creature
lives. I wonder more what it knows about our world.*

– Kenneth Gross, *Puppet: An Essay on Uncanny Life*

Contents

III

I

The Archeology of the Dollhouse

No pet so obedient. No scene
so unchanging. Diorama
of a vanished civilization.

We put our heads together.
We pull up our sleeves and go in,

fingers broaching a window,
chubby fists rappelling walls.

Boxes

The dollhouse is a box
like most things,
a tooth, a heart, a tomb.
Cloud glory crowns it
or it is maybe struck
by eyeball-shaped hail.
At dusk, the earth's shadow
falls over it. The dollhouse
is an ecosystem with
a fixed population.
Their wool-strand hair.
Their wooden feet.
They find themselves
stretched out on the sofa
or folded into a chair
by a window,
gaze directed out.
Gabled and balconied
the dollhouse clings
like a shoe. A refuge
is what it is.
A destination.
Even the smallest
can say the address.

Made of Clay

The house is not wooden, not even
plastic. Precariously, it is made of clay.
The walls meet at right angles as they would
in a real house. The broad blank spaces
face one another, as if in defiance. Clay,
but it could as easily be a gingerbread house,
crumbling if shaken. The people, dolls,
installed here, take care, walk softly, supported
by our fingers. The house resembles an enchanted castle—
enter and you are changed. Maybe you will fall
asleep. Maybe you will remain forever.

Lady and Man

There must be a lady and a man.
They will be the mommy and daddy.
The toilet and the dining table
are sized for them. Children, if included,
are fractions of the originals.
They will grow into the allotted spaces,
but in the meantime must be aware
of gaps in the plank floor,
taking care not to fall through.

The lady wears a dress protected
by a flowered apron. Her stockings
and high-heeled shoes taper
to feet dainty as deer hooves.

The man is bigger, with wide shoulders.
He pulls a tie like a noose over the collar
of his button-down shirt. With him,
he carries a briefcase that he exchanges
for a newspaper as soon as he can.

At home, he makes himself comfortable
beneath a tasseled floor lamp,
accommodating himself to the green
velvet armchair. Sometimes the lady
and the man are in the same room
at the same time but this is not necessary.

Empty Rooms

This is a three-bedroom dollhouse,
and with a 2.1 replacement rate
for the nation's population, there are
only two doll children, disregarding
the other .1. Some of the rooms
are therefore at all times empty.
For instance, everyone goes away
in the morning. The mother, first back,
has been only as far as the market
and brings home what they will need
to make it through the day: white sandwich bread,
spreads to put in the middle that glue
the slices together, soft cakes, soda.
At lunch, the children come home to be fed,
fueled for the return to school.
The daddy is gone longest. In the day
they all use the kitchen and dining
and living rooms and at night, fill up
the bedrooms until the next morning
when the circuit begins again.

Mischief

The boy's striped polo shirt and short pants
are attached to him. The girl is modeled
after the lady, the same red fruit for lips.
Her short pink dress ties in back and Mary Janes
grip her folded-over white anklets.
Together, the little dolls are mischievous
and pull the cat doll's tail. They thump, thump
down the steps on their bottoms or slide
the banister. They get in the way
of the man and lady. It is too many dolls,
sometimes, despite the empty rooms.

Whose dollhouse?

It was Sandra's, where we played, meant to keep her company while her mother went off to work, so she could see how a real family lived. My only doll was a hand-me-down. A pillow for a belly and eyes that moved like shutters going up and down. My mother knew real babies come soon enough. But the facts of life are different for dolls: some mistake in the mix and match of chromosomes. They'll never reproduce but trading off, they won't get old. I named my beat-up doll Lily, for Sandra's mother, not my own.

On Site

Where they live, at the top of the hill,
the woods pile up behind them. A sound
of trees all around, like someone swinging
on a door. In the walls there's an autumn chill,
even on hottest days, even as the trillium opens
like the beaks of baby birds. The lady
likes to sweep up dust and the open side
makes it easy.

             We have furnished the dollhouse
piece by piece, installing a sofa with bumpy
upholstery that dots the sitter's back.
The cat curls on a shag rug the size
of a stamp. Everyone's socks, rolled into balls,
rest in the same bureau drawer.
Night drops over the dollhouse
like the cover on a canary cage.

The Boy, the Girl

Throughout the house,
you smell the lady's lily scent.
The man doll is shiny surfaced
and sturdy. The boy and girl,
—their parents refer to them
as the boy, the girl—are small,
vivid creatures, with bright eyes.

For such is family: the four of them
in short sleeves, dressed always
for summer, listening
to what surrounds them,
chants of insects, the threat of rain.

The Importance of the Dollhouse

It is the only safe place for them.
Tiny birds clack in the backyard
and wild animals prowl the alley.
When we play, we sometimes take
the dollhouse on our laps, but things inside
tend to tilt or fall, what isn't fixed down.
The furniture throws proportional
shadows as in a real house. The little girl
must wear white cotton underpants. On this,
the mommy is clear, and she has been told
never to let a boy pull them down.
Also, there will be no leaning
against walls, even to remain upright.
Outside is a gate which requires a key
and police not far off, even soldiers.

I may see myself passing through
the little house, the clay house of myself,
walking quickly past the windows.

Picnic

They are on a hill far away picnicking.
They eat soft cake and pour lemonade.
A chenille bedspread undulates under them.

But where is the chair to lean on as you rise?
Where the bathtub shaped around you like an egg cup?

Everything in the open has achieved
a state of uncertainty. And if they go back
to the house (they must go back to the house)
that is something tangible or at the least,
a center to whatever kaleidoscope
pulls the sky around in circles.

Rain

It rains and they hurry home.
In the rain the dollhouse grows dark.
Lightning cracks the sky into pieces,
and drops streak the windows. Even so,
it is cozy. The children do their lessons
on checkered oilcloth at the kitchen table.
The cat and the refrigerator purr.
Soup bubbles and clouds the air.
The soup pot, set on the stovetop,
doesn't of course come off, but the family
pretends. The soup is green with things
that are good for you, so the little dolls
try not to eat it. It gets saved
from day to day until it is gone.

You could stitch a sweater from
the strands of rain that circle them.
The downpour may be permanent.

Night and Day

What would they do without night
to cut apart the days? Without even
the interference of the rain? Sometimes
the lady cries at night. If the others listened,
they could hear. She looks out her window
for the star that lies on its side as she does,
spraying light. At dark we clean up dolls
and furniture. Everything fits into the square boxes
of rooms, swept together with our hands.
Even vases and flowers, tilted, overturned. Order
to be restored when we play again tomorrow.

Nightmares

How could you not have them?
Exposed as you are, always,
on the one side. Who is watching?

There are prayers before sleep
as though they were all undertaking
a great journey. Probably they are.

For you walk and walk in your dreams,
the ground giving way underneath.
And what of the man in the cellar?

The doll children are afraid that
they have not prayed hard enough.
Therefore, they put off the night as long
as they can. Weighted down by flannel,

they whisper through the thin wall
that separates their connected sleep.

Secrets

Somewhere fingernails are being
clipped, staccato, not at all equal.
You can hear this but not the growth
of them in the first place, or of hair.
The oven stays shut and mouths
aren't meant to open. Parts of dolls
are soiled or worn where human
children press. Anything in the world
that happens leaves a mark. The dolls
are always being picked up and placed
by forces outside their control.
Words are put into their mouths.

Piano Lesson

Music gives, music is fluid,
music lets you fit words in.
Is there music in the dollhouse?

At 4 a gray-haired lady
comes to sit beside first the girl
then the boy. Her middle is stiff
with the corset she wears under her silky,
pleated dress. The child-fingers cover
only half the keys and don't reach far.
The teacher shows them how,
and that they can't hope to equal her.

Lace bibs her throat and she hums
as they repeat a phrase, even a note,
giving them the path of her perfect pitch.
If they knew the pain she was in
as she perches there. One pain
or another that she holds to herself.
It is hard work. It is hard to walk or sit,
habits though they are. But in the life
of the body, hearing is the last sense to go.

Excluded

Because she sat on the door step
and her mother wasn't there.
No One was there. The key
on a string around her neck, tied to her,
key to a whole world, gone. An uninhabited
interior. Her paint set. Warm milk.

Would she be taken in? Nothing,
she now knew, she wanted so much.
The color of the moment, relentless,
indomitable. Like the piano notes
she had scattered with small fingers
into the cosmos. Lost, as she was lost.
Her family, even fighting, the raised voices,
syllables of long duration.

She must be bad. Once, she had a home.
Even a bird has a home, a place it belongs,
in a tree. For dolls, it's a dollhouse.
Though wind sometimes throws
a nestling to the ground for no reason.

We Play Teatime in the Dollhouse

Social Tea Biscuits and Lipton's,
blue willow saucers and cups.

The blue is ink, telling the story,
the white is the empty page.

A girl is locked in a garden. Seasons
and roses, even thrushes taunt her.

But the wall is the wall of her childhood.
All day she walks beside water

through lilies and weeping trees.
Then someone, he must be the prince,

approaches, and in a steam of longing,
they kiss and fly away, birds.

We each pinch a tiny cup handle,
pinky raised in the air like a tail.

Dollhouse Ways

Anyhow, the dollhouse dolls
are capable of certain gestures.
For instance, to pace the tiny rooms
(we always count the footsteps to a wall)
or stiffly raise their arms in consternation.

The ethics of the dollhouse are that
a person should be good and pleasant and kind.

One day the girl doll will marry
her high school sweetheart,
that handsome boy with leather elbows
and a number on his back. A known quantity,
as she is, who sings doo-wop
and has been vetted by the school.

The House Speaks

Girl:

I love our maid, Lorilene.
I wish she was my mom.
She is always cracking gum
and singing. Somewhere she has
her own house, her own hidden children.
Who takes care of them?

Boy:

The grown-ups. When do they do
the secret things? Everyone
has a secret. Or else why
are there bathroom doors?

Lady:

I want to make them love me.
I know, I'll bake a chocolate cake.
There is no written down recipe
but I have it by heart. Duncan Hines
and sour cream in a bundt pan.

Man:

Tonight I'll take them to the top
of the hill. No one around.
Of course, it will scare them.
The moon so bright,
as we lie on the grass and wait
for planets to fall or UFOs.

The Dollhouse:

Empty, I am lonely. But at day's end
the dolls come back from life. Life is not easy,
especially when you are frightened and tiny.

I'm fond of them. The girl doll
has a little girl doll she makes speak French.
As for the father, he worries so.
Even if you get insurance do you think
it can keep bad things from happening?

What of the man in the cellar?

The Lady of the House Fills Her Day

after 8 hours sleep
a bath
a novel
a manual of instructions,
the Frigidaire muttering
3 x tv
3 x tooth brushing
listening for mail
1 x, mail whispered through slot
what to open, what to throw away
put on stockings and shoes
take them off
put on slippers
take off slippers
put on stockings and shoes
a nap
a walk
cook breakfast
prepare lunch
get dinner ready
look out window
autumn is so metallic
watch as it brightens and shatters
wait for everyone
turn on radio
turn off radio
fetch newspaper
check obits and movie listings
cut out articles of life interest
file appropriately: those

pertaining to health insurance,
under health insurance
talk on telephone if someone calls
sit

Girl: Bicameral

Two ways of looking, left and right.
Two eyes two arms two legs.
The same apparatus whichever way
you turn. As a man reading the paper
when spoken to lifts up his head,
a woman, drawing the pot to a boil,
faces only one way, down.

A boy, a girl/ a cat, a dog. Everything
in the dollhouse, in perfect balance.
Two windows, each with a view of its own,
above the open mouth of a door.

Sunshine or rain. Out or in. Night
not day. Good or bad. Forget then remember.
School, and after, home. So many choices,
or two at least. Sitting vs. standing. Poor
vs. rich, young and old. Alive/dead.
black/white. But also, and here I throw up
my hands, grey, grey, grey.

II

Geometry

The dollhouse is a lesson in geometry,
squares and rectangles cut apart
and reassembled to facilitate movement.

Cold, this intent, and hard-angled.
But the people who live here exude the light
of their industry. Their energetic longing.
Sighs and warm breath. And the squares

and rectangles fill with the scents
of pots on the stove, of onion and cinnamon.
Afternoons, piano notes bounce off the walls,
the fingering of children practicing their scales.

Plants garnish the living room, and the animals
that live inside the people express their meaning,
anger and sorrow, coming and going,
multiplied in the fantasies of mirrors.

Family Portrait

Of course, they want to be like everyone.
The way the fangblenny alters its spots,
or the caterpillar masquerades as a twig.

The way, in fact, fifty species of moths
and butterflies at some point in their lives
conceal themselves to keep from being eaten.

As always, they walk out together
with the same lidded eyes, the same archaic
half-smile that draws up their cheekbones.

"No affect" is a family characteristic.
The point, not to broadcast your feelings,
not to be noticed, to make no impression.

When the boy's teacher writes home,
"Does not exert himself," he knows she means
"assert," and that he's doing something right.

This day, the family steps out. All their faces flatten
onto a snapshot, elbows scratched
in the same place in their hurry to get back in.

I locate my nine-year-old self.

In the picture, I know where to look
for me, sullen and uncomfortable
in a satin party dress, between
my mother and father and against
my brother, who is always concocting
some test of whether I should be allowed
to exist. I pick at a scab
that ornaments my wrist. The pain
is a memorial to a time I was whole,
though I know the split will join,
will become nearly invisible.

Everything belongs to me.

I can go into any drawer
of the polished breakfront
with its wide mirror that looks back at me
and not be surprised.
Here, beside linen and forks,
the prayer books I hesitate to touch are laid,
letters rising up like flame.

In summertime
the imitation oriental rugs
are switched for straw.
Then moonlight dots the trees
and the porch light flares
with its satellite bugs. Brother,

I write you in. Other people
only pass the time. You make things happen.
Torments of yours in darkened rooms:
You scratch and pinch.
You jump out and scare me.
You tell me one day
I must die. All this, long, long before
the house I remember us in is gone.

Stairway

Think of the dollhouse
as a collection, a museum,
even a prison. But a little doll,
a tiny chair, mean nothing
if not in the context of a house.

Though here there is,
I don't know, despite its protection,
such capacity for movement, change.

At night, for instance, a house
talks back, crackles and knocks.

Turn on the alarm and it is like
setting the alarm of your fear,
little birdcall of eternity.

Downstairs you have only just
shut the door on the world
and you float up, giddy with sleep.

You fly—don't they call the sets
of steps flights? And at the top,
massive dark winds through the hall.

No one is safe. But you open a door,
look through a window
and there it is, pocketed by the sky,
the nearly perfect moon.

The Greater Doll Family

Dolls that shriek when you squeeze
or shake one way and then
the other,
sound going forward and back, wa-aw,

Those whose lips form an O
you thread
with the nipple of a tiny bottle,
"drink me," liquid leaking out their bottom.

Others with rubber arms,
slick and cool,
as they wrap around your neck.

Some whose hair you can wash.
Some with a dimple
at their very middle for a belly button.

Dolls even at school, stiff
little figures you lay to sleep
in a Junior Red Cross box
alongside bandaids and barrettes

that are meant
to be sent off to children
after war.

Madonna of the Dollhouse

A missionary in the park
gave us this card, a painting
to hang on the dollhouse wall.

The Virgin Mary sits, prayers in hand,
amid the pillars of her invisible room.

Dove and announcing angel
flutter into view. The belly of her dress
with its delicate floral embroidery
is slit like a surgery
so the Holy Spirit can come in.

Hidden

Our dollhouse of course has in it
a dollhouse. Otherwise, how to provide
recreation for the children? Or maybe
the boy will prefer a model railroad
where the house is one of the stops.
It could take invalids to the doll hospital
and deliver them home, rehabilitated.

We who play here must speak softly
and miniaturize our emotions.
The landscape insinuates itself
around the train, rising up, up,
as if all the land above water aspired
to be a mountain. The shape
of a head in the engine room must
undoubtedly be a head.

Cat

She comes
on little cat feet.

Everyone knows
all cats are girls,
all dogs are boys.

The cat knows
how to know things
with her breath, her mouth,
her paws.
She knows to allow
herself to be petted
because she is a pet.

She even knows
she is a cat
in a dollhouse, that all this
is make believe.

Man: Chewing Gum

I had to find the right tool
and rummaged in the drawer.
Metal, maybe, like a screw driver
but not wanting to muddle a screw
driver, they have so clear
a use, and coming up at last
with a thin piece of blue plastic.
What had I saved it for but this?
A rhomboid shape with a hollowed
center, meant maybe to shape
other rhomboids if you'd ever
want to do that. And I scraped
with its one short side the gum
that had transferred from my shoe
to the wood plank floor of the living room.
Then I sprayed the gooey residue
with Fantastic as any other man I know
has learned to do, a gesture
of cleaning.

Jump Rope Song

Please, Mr. Crocodile,
may we cross the water
to see your lovely daughter?

Once, Mr. Crocodile,
in the night we sought her,
hearing her sweet laughter.
It was your daughter we were after.

Yes, we are, I am,
wearing something blue.

Dear Mr. Crocodile,
Is it true you've lost her?
Then let us cross the water.

When we have caught her,
we'll toss her up to you again
in a golden cup and saucer.

Neighbor: Let Me Be!

Some random person,
Ms. Barber? Ms. Beaver?
rode by my house. Don't
know who or when. Can't
be expected to keep track of dates.
And those people I'd have to
meet over again to remember.
But one afternoon they rode by
in a slow car, sent one random boy,
maybe the next door boy,
out with an envelope to slip
in my mail slot in my door.
I never heard the chink of the flap.
Probably I was not home
so could not cuss whoever out.
Invitation? Contamination!

III

If it was

those years ago
it would have been
the beach, the beach
or the lake.
It would have been
night, been my brother
or my lover. Silver Lake.
The night, the lake,
a double darkness
but one side shone.
Swans in a row
and inside,
people dancing.
Or else it was the beach.
Sand, of course,
and you paid to swim.
It would have been
96 in the city
but out here I shivered
where my limbs
were bare. If it
was my brother,
I knew him, however
obliquely, as birches
lean together, grow,
the way a sister
knows her brother.
I scarcely knew
my lover. Only
at night, in the moon

in the park, on a porch.
So shy I couldn't
speak, like water
that stretches
over sand and pulls away.
If it was my brother,
one swim, cooling,
and the slow ride home.

"Huguette Clark: Reclusive Heiress"

1. Porcelain Doll

From my mother I have my name
and the fine French dolls
presented to me as a child.

From my father, 121 rooms of my own house,
five other homes if I'd care to go.
A rapid heartbeat, unsettling dreams.

2. Doll Love

Not the affection among dolls,
if they could love. That would be
fellow creature love, sentimental attachment.
This is more, if you will, transgressive.
Love of a child, even a grown person,
for the image of itself. So, heiress, divorcee
of a perhaps unconsummated marriage,
Huguette Clark devoted herself
to Vintage dolls in their thirty houses
in the biggest apartment on Fifth Avenue.

They couldn't of course love back,
snuggle against her thighs like a cat.
But she liked their helplessness and
their cool precision. Had her housekeeper
iron their clothes. She spoke for them
in high, imagined voices. At dinner
sat them down beside her. And afterward
would lay them in their own tiny beds,
in their intricate, pleated frocks.
She was never alone. Even in sleep,
doll eyes open, staring back at her.

3. The Cloister of Hospitals

For 30 years I hid in the bed's
farthest corner. I hid in another name,
above the shiny streets of a winter thaw
where I couldn't be caught in myself
and held somehow for ransom.

Fed and cleaned, bundled in care,
I'd wait for a comforting voice
above the air-conditioning,
and medicine if they thought I needed it.

The day revolved like the black
clock hand, shadow circling
the white room. Upright like a doll
in my chair, reading a book or parsing
through the window, an alphabet of lights.

Boy: Wolfman

"Even if you are
pure in heart and say your prayers by night
you may become a wolf
when the woolfbane blooms
and the autumn moon is bright."
—gypsies in the movie, "The Wolf Man"

Do you believe in Werewolves? I do.
I saw in this movie the moon
open up to someone its fullness, its possibility.
And after, how he arrived at his first face
of the morning, revived
from the madness of sleep.

He left a little trail of blood
from the nightly kill.
He became an animal
and had no shame or strategy,
an animal's dearth of excuses.

They say, if your eyebrows nearly meet
it could be a sign you're a werewolf.
But in that case, you can be cured
if someone should call you
by your own given name three times.

Otherwise, only a weapon of silver
will end the spell. In the movie a man
thrashes the wolf
with a silver-headed cane,
surprised when the dying creature
melts back into his son.

Found

*My father drops the little brown leather memorandum book,
edges foxed and feathered with use. Gray pencil dusts the
pages like a shadow of his own demise. Only names and
columns of numbers, captured in their prison of lines, where
he borrows from the future, gives away the past. And all of it
flattens to a rubber band in his jacket pocket. Messages to
himself, reminding what is owed him by the world.*

Man: Father

How we hold on. How we connect,
know that the large protect the small,

as this small bird is carried along
in the hawk's airstream.

And I want to explain to them,
the girl, the boy,
what they and I together see. I need
to find an explanation.

Later too, as Venus dangles
from the invisible hand of the moon,

and orphan stars flash out
in their search for a parent planet.

Orion

We are out on a winter night, searching
for Orion. The only light's the moon.

A fattening moon but still it's dark down here
beyond our bright house, dark.

In oversize mukluks we pack down the snow,
crushed crystal like the granular surface of the moon.

Animal stars hunch down beside the moon
into the folds of their black velvet diagram

in fear of Orion, stealthy hunter, stalker.
The moon connects to us by a long, icy rope.

Once in moonlight, I watched the big
unrestrained snowball of a comet fall.

Yet even here I'm mooning over losses, despite
appearances, despite my children, and the full night sky.

Dollmaker: First Try

I wander into the sculpture class,
a dozen aged or aging women
confronting stone. I think,
They are looking at their tombstones.
Yet in a week I too am fumbling
with a boulder half my weight.

The rock offers nothing, blank
as wall. But neither is it dead matter.
It is thinking its own thoughts:
winter afternoon, sun-smudged window,
iced threads of a spider web. At every
hammerstroke the blow comes back to me.

Now sun ignites the alabaster grain.
I am glad for this, a dawn I can use.
Through the dove shape of my working hands
I inch forward, until one day
a smooth arm pushes away
from the stone chest, freeing itself.

The Dollmaker at Work

Here, shelved,
         anywhere I look,
the unfinished faces of dolls.

        Bodies will be added
            and after, clothes.

        You ask yourself
if the doll duplicates you
        or if you have re-invented yourself
            in the perfect shape of the doll.

And all along you need to know
what the doll
        is pretending to be.

            *

Twisting clay, forming it,
        you make a plea
for its resurrection.
        For the doll is arrested life.

        Anything left over,
      return
to formlessness
        so you can begin again.

            *

The work is best done
in borrowed light: skylight, fanlight,
light from the window
of an adjoining room.

At dawn
or in the purple aftermath
of sunset.

*

The doll breaks as you might break.

Expect accidents.
Air bubbles,
a list to its side as it bakes.
The unintentioned painful crease
under a fourth toe.

Too frail elbows, bowed legs.

*

But when the doll wakes
to the iced breath
of the world
goodness shines
from the enameled eyes.

Yes, yes, the doll says.
All it can say, Yes.

A guest

The rat, sluggish and wary,
with fur like the dust of the world,
slinked into our street from the sewer
that edged the corner. I knew
it had come for me. It climbed
the surface of every door in turn,
feet spread, attempting entry.
Confused, out in the open. Yellow door,
red door, imagining what it had left,
where next it would be accepted.

Girl: Little Figure in Landscape

This is not a trustworthy day,
that squint of lightning, rain any minute.
Soon the sun will bleed out of the sky,
leaving black trees and a darkness
that conceals animals. If I could take apart
the view and put it back another way—

It starts with something I hear.
A rat in the basement? The meter reader?
How could he get in?

Maybe the agency for maids
has sent a substitute,
a big woman in a kerchief
who later changes into her—his—own men's clothes.

I know I'm beckoned with a flashlight,
chloroformed cloth pressed
against my streaming face. I am flung
like laundry into someone's backseat.

Later, let go, wandering, I breathe in
the cool, leafed smell of summer.
Grass happens, and bracken. Sky
edges through the trees like shards
of broken mirror. I'm afraid. I don't know
how much of outside a little figure can withstand.

There would have been a door to open
and walk through, a corner to be turned

where you could see the moon
hung out to dry, the mountain ridge

like blue felt, like an ink-saturated blotter.
Pink moon, moon of the flowers.

Oh, break me apart from sleep.
Let me go off into empty streets
where the forest
of 22 irreconcilable shades of green
stops. On blades of grass,
white butterflies coloring
or is it only
the green I keep in my eye,
with deer, a weasel, true-hearted violets?

And I wonder, have they forgotten me?
Do I not belong to our house anymore?
They, with all the space in the world,
still hovering together. The dream
is driving me on, convincing me
of a world airy and soulless, an illusion.
Not me, away, not me,
until I come back to myself.

Travelers

1.

The earth won't stop,
plates incessantly moving

and planets are wanderers,
the sky tonight expanding,
contracting, so much energy

that I take comfort in sleep.
Travel is exhausting.

A planet is a round thing
that winds around a star.

Its orbit is a kind of invisible
string, as a string winds around

a yoyo. Maybe stars want displacement.
Maybe they believe as we do

when we take a trip that love and riches
are waiting somewhere to receive us.

2.

The dolls, do they crave displacement?
Would they like to travel?

Are they too convinced somewhere else
good fortune is waiting
to receive them?

When they are jumbled in mid-play
by clumsy fingers into boxes,

are they aware they are dolls
in a dollhouse, miniature and lost
to meaning, not free to choose?

Do they question what lies
outside themselves,

afraid those wanderers,
the planets, looking down at them,
see into their tiny hearts?

War

Wasn't the dollhouse the lady's theater
of operations? She, like all of them,
with her head larger than life. Staunch
in the flowered apron as an epauletted
general. She swore her husband
was not stationed here. That this
was not his address. In fact, that he spent
his entire life somewhere else.
The doorframe trembled when he arrived.
He left on that side his dog tag and true identity.
Typically he came for R and R,
not even knowing the rules, where
the forks go, what time school let out.

Theater

In the doll drama there must be
conflict, tension between what's socially
accepted and what the doll wants to do,
like going out without clothes.

The actors, in this case, family,
share a dialogue. "I want" and
"You can't have." For instance
"I want to go to the party," and
"Not if the parents aren't home."

"I intend to build a bomb shelter
under the basement." "Nuh-uh. The city
would have to give us permission."

Remember the silence of the theater.
Newton's idea of space, an empty stage.
The void the actors' words must leap across
into the ears of the audience
who in the dark eagerly await them.

And sometimes the stage manager,
here, imagine her the mother,
looks out and says, "The house is
half-empty tonight." Where are the others?
Is it worth it to start a row?

Like family, the purpose of plot
is to connect the characters. People
bound together in close relationship.

A simple plot involves a change
of fortune: "Well, children, Daddy
has a gambling addiction. So I guess
it's working the checkout instead
of college." There might also
be the pathos of a fatal or harmful act.
"I am taking a lover as they do in France,
and I would like him to live here with us.
He can help carry groceries."

All the while the ensemble, absurd
as the words might be, must speak
with clarity and emphasis
to express the force of emotion
that underlies each line.

The director—that's us—first explains
to them the purpose of their speech,
not for a moment should they step
out of character, whatever they are painted,
even formed to represent.

For instance, we've come to know
the father as an amateur astronomer
who searches the fields for UFO's,
the boy as a child drawn to monsters,
and the girl, the only one yet
to have met the man in the cellar.

Mr. & Mrs. Peter Doll Invite You to an Open House

1.

Welcome to our grand Victorian mansion.
All the rooms, lit from within. So much
brought to life, in each a figure, stationed,
facing you, or as if a doll, a pet,
has just left, the chess board set for a game,
a banjo or guitar, silent for the moment,
propped against a chair. Even the secret room
at the top, though you couldn't see through
a closed door in the wall, is occupied.
It might be one of the ten children,
four of whom are two sets of twins.
Or, also on site, one of five servants,
among them scullery and parlor maids,
a valet. And many pets: dog, cat,
canary, and a family of white rats.
In the evening, often, fireworks
for some reason, leap into the sky.
Think of their visibility,
unmistakable, though only 4%
of the universe is visible.
Lost elsewhere in the scenery,
for instance, the spark struck off two stones.
A figure at each window then, eager, looking out.

2.

Mr. D, still in his robe, rubbing sleep
from his eyes, sits clipping coupons
at his desk. In the newspaper soon
he will trace the rising silhouette
of his stocks. Mrs. D is already
planning the dinner menu
while a seamstress embraces,
with dimity and pins, her equivalent
form in the sewing room. Above stairs
a servant empties slops. And from below
comes the rhythm of moist diapers
slapped against a scrub board in a tub.
America is just rolling out of bed.
America is forging steel, confining
working children to factories
or depositing them in shadowy mines.
America is making a buck, showing itself
to the world like a full set of teeth.

3.

Real Estate consists of 1.32 ac. m/l rectangular lot whereon is
erected a 23-rm., 4 sty. Victorian estate w/adjoining carriage hse.
Mature shrubs, fruiting and blossoming, surround dwelling.
Mature trees, uniformly spaced, shade lawn. Ent. leads to foyer
w/coat closet. Kitchen has cherry paneling, w. attached pantry,
w/w carpeted D.R., adjacent fam. rm. L.R. w. bookshelves on
either side of brick F.P. Lg. enclosed brick patio/sunroom. Upper
fls.: five B.R.'s, each w. own cedar-lined walk-in closet. Master
B.R. incl. full bath. Study, sewing room, two nurseries. Sm. ser-
vant rooms and trunk room in attic. Full finished basement has
cement fl., full equipped laundry w. washtubs. 2 stairwys, front and
bk., carved wd. newel posts. Indoor plumb. On-site well and sep-
tic. Property well-cared for, in immaculate cond., ready to move
in. Owners have vacated for small apt. and are motivated to sell.

Collector

A doll is an object, a trinket, a token.
Yet the dolls are not collected
in a glass case, which would remove them
from their main function, life.

Instead, they inhabit a dollhouse,
based on our memory
of the real. In them we recover our history.

They take us inside ourselves,
stripping layer after layer
to bone or soul,
to our own object smoothness.

They do what we have them do.
They are engaged, peeling potatoes,
unzipping the tiny pods of peas.
Like us, they take a pill to make
something happen, or not happen.

On the other hand,
we are always serving the doll.
Its open eyes, its open mouth.
The collector collects
to give the dolls their freedom.

The Collection

Collected: so many smiles.
You visit with the dolls, then turn away.
And because they are toys,
they allow themselves to be toyed with.

In your fingers you chafe the dolls
as if for luck. Always gently,
so as not to leave a mark.
They are accustomed to being
stared at, weighed in your hands.

Otherwise, the dolls sit.
Calm skin that never warms.
For you and for them, collecting
is about waiting. A collection
is never really complete.

Collectible

For under stress, don't we attempt
even to collect ourselves?
Oh, I want to be with the dolls,
shuffling through their three-sided rooms
that are open to everyone,
perky round fruit laid in bowls,
flowers poking up from tables.
Where they dress to go out
or relinquish themselves to sleep.
Where they know what to do.

Acknowledgments

Earlier versions of some of these poems appear in the following magazines: *Hotel Amerika*: "Boxes," "The Boy, the Girl," "Man: Father," and "Girl: Little Figure in Landscape"; *Blue Lyra*: "Stairway"; *Pleiades*: "Geometry."

Meditations on houses and rooms, the spaces that define us, owe much to Bachelard's *The Poetics of Space*.

Susan Stewart's *On Longing* is a haunting, beautiful book and helped me visualize the power in miniatures.

"Script," a memorable poem by Mark Halliday, offered a format for "The House Speaks."

Stardate's radio spots on PBS brought some authenticity to the man's interest in outer space, including "the fattening moon."

The story of Huguette Clark and her love of dolls was told in an obituary by Magalit Fox in *The New York Times* (May 25, 2011), "Huguette Clark, Reclusive Heiress, Dies at 104."

"Boy: Wolfman" relates to the horror movie of that name starring Lon Chaney as a protagonist who is victim as much as predator.

"Mr. and Mrs. Peter Doll Invite You to an Open House." Details from *America's Dollhouse: The Miniature World of Faith Bradford* by William L. Bird, Jr. (Princeton Architectural Press, 2010).

The last poems, on collecting, were inspired by Walter Benjamin's essays in *Illuminations* and elsewhere and on the miniature ceramic rooms and furniture of Harry Cummings.

Thanks to Jeanne Murray Walker who made insightful comments about poems all along the way and other friends, particularly Sharon White.

"Jump Rope Song" is based on a game of English schoolchildren, noted on the website www.projectbritain.com, Playground Games.

Also, I am grateful to Nicola Cooperman, Alexa and Samantha Block, and Lisa and Dana Goldblatt for access to their dollhouses.

Elaine Terranova is the author of five books of poems and
two chapbooks. Her work has appeared in a number of liter-
ary magazines and anthologies. Her translation of Euripides'
Iphigenia at Aulis is part of the Penn Greek Drama Series.
She has received the Walt Whitman Award, an NEA, a Pew
Fellowship, and a Pushcart Prize.